C. Sq., Sp.,
pg. 38

SPORT SHORT
One low point in Manchester United's history occurred in February 1958. Eight players were killed in a plane crash, and several others were hurt. Sir Matt Busby, the team's manager, or coach, at the time was among those hurt in the crash.

Manchester United players (in pearl) celebrate winning an important match against French team Paris Saint-Germain (in black) in 2016.

Introducing Manchester United FC 11

...G LEVEL: 5 / INTEREST LEVEL: 5-8

	PRINT ISBN	eBOOK ISBN	©	GRL	DEWEY	ATOS
	978-1-5026-5308-6					
...ona Young-Brown)	978-1-5026-5268-3	978-1-5026-5269-0	©2020	T	796.33	PENDING
...nich (Derek Miller)	978-1-5026-5277-5	978-1-5026-5278-2	©2020	T	796.334	
...United FC (Cathleen Small)	978-1-5026-5265-2	978-1-5026-5266-9	©2020	T	796.33	PENDING
...ermain FC (Kate Shoup)	978-1-5026-5286-7	978-1-5026-5287-4	©2020	T	796.33	
Real Madrid CF (Kate Shoup)	978-1-5026-5262-1	978-1-5026-5263-8	©2020	T	796.33	PENDING

Library Binding • 64 pp. • 6" x 9" • Black-and-White and Full-Color Photographs • Biographies • Fact Boxes • Glossary • Index • Sidebars

Each Book: $34.21/$23.95 • 5-Book Set: $171.05/$119.75

D1512072

SOCCER'S
Greatest Clubs

Manchester United FC

Cathleen Small

Cavendish
Square

New York

Published in 2020 by Cavendish Square Publishing, LLC
243 5th Avenue, Suite 136, New York, NY 10016

Copyright © 2020 by Cavendish Square Publishing, LLC

First Edition

Website: cavendishsq.com

This publication represents the opinions and views of the author based on
his or her personal experience, knowledge, and research. The information
in this book serves as a general guide only. The author and publisher have
used their best efforts in preparing this book and disclaim liability rising
directly or indirectly from the use and application of this book.

All websites were available and accurate when this book was sent to press.

Library of Congress Cataloging-in-Publication Data

Names: Small, Cathleen, author.
Title: Manchester United FC / Cathleen Small.
Other titles: Manchester United Football Club
Description: First edition. | New York : Cavendish Square, 2020. | Series: Soccer's greatest
clubs | Audience: Grades: 5 to 8. | Includes bibliographical references and index.
Identifiers: LCCN 2019015204 (print) | LCCN 2019019419 (ebook) | ISBN 9781502652669
(ebook) | ISBN 9781502652652 (library bound) | ISBN 9781502652645 (pbk.)
Subjects: LCSH: Manchester United (Soccer team)--Juvenile literature.
| Soccer teams--England--Manchester--Juvenile literature.
Classification: LCC GV943.6.M3 (ebook) | LCC GV943.6.M3
S63 2020 (print) | DDC 796.334/640942733--dc23
LC record available at https://lccn.loc.gov/2019015204

Editor: Kristen Susienka
Copy Editor: Rebecca Rohan
Associate Art Director: Alan Sliwinski
Designer: Joe Parenteau
Production Coordinator: Karol Szymczuk
Photo Research: J8 Media

Printed in the United States of America

TABLE OF CONTENTS

Chapter 1:
Introducing Manchester United FC . . . 5

Chapter 2:
The Beginning 13

Chapter 3:
An Offering of Awards and Accolades . .27

Chapter 4:
Challenges for the Club 37

Chapter 5:
Manchester United's Future 49

Chronology 55
Glossary 57
Further Information 59
Selected Bibliography 61
Index 63
About the Author 64

Manchester United players celebrate after scoring a goal in a 2019 match against the Wolverhampton Wanderers.

INTRODUCING MANCHESTER UNITED FC

Soccer is not the most popular sport in the United States. It is also not the most popular sport in Canada, though it is gaining more fans there. Many people would say football, baseball, hockey, and basketball are the more popular sports in these two countries. However, in the rest of the world, soccer is very popular. The Super Bowl, the biggest game in American football, usually has around 150 million viewers, but the World Cup, which features the biggest matches in soccer, has more than 1 billion viewers!

FOOTBALL OR SOCCER?

England may be a small country, but like much of the world, the English—and many others in Great Britain— love soccer. They call it football, just like many other countries do.

The word "soccer" actually comes from British English, not American English, but the British don't often use it when talking about the sport. Because the United States and several other countries (such as Canada,

Ireland, and Australia) have other popular sports already called football, they call this sport "soccer."

A LITTLE HISTORY

In England, "football" was originally a mix of what is now rugby and what is now soccer. In 1863, the sports began to split off and create different sports organizations, or associations. The Football Association in England became the governing body of soccer. It made the game's first rules. A few years later, rugby started a governing body called the Rugby Football Union. That meant the two sports were no longer connected.

The Northampton Town Football Club team poses for a picture during the 1897–1898 season.

The soccer clubs began to play under the Football Association. In 1872, the first soccer competition was created. It was called the Football Association Challenge Cup (today the FA Cup). That same year, England played Scotland in the first international soccer match. In 1888, the first soccer league was formed in England, with twelve clubs. Today, it is called the English Football League, with seventy-two teams.

When international soccer matches became more common, the International Football Association Board (IFAB) was formed. It began to agree on the laws of the game. In 1904, Féderation Internationale de Football Association (FIFA), the international governing body of soccer, started. FIFA now publishes the laws of soccer—all seventeen of them. However, IFAB is the body that carries out the laws, as well as other agreements that help the game of soccer stay the same every season.

MANCHESTER UNITED FOOTBALL CLUB

Manchester United began as part of the English Football League, but it is now part of the Premier League. The Premier League split off from the English Football League in 1992.

A RAILWAY CLUB

Manchester United has existed for more than 140 years—before the first soccer league was formed in England. However, it wasn't always called Manchester United. When the club began in 1878, it was Newton Heath LYR Football Club. (LYR stands for Lancashire and Yorkshire Railway.) However, by 1902 the club was named Manchester United. It has been so ever since.

Manchester United's full name is Manchester United Football Club, but it is also known as simply Manchester United, Man U, or just United. Some people also call the team the Red Devils.

Manchester United is extremely well known, even to people who don't know a lot about soccer. The reason is probably because the club has been very successful. It has won more titles and cups than any other club in English soccer. In recent years, it has also had the highest earnings of any soccer club in the world. This is partly due to the club's brand and the business opportunities it brings—a successful club usually also has lots of sponsors and a good reputation.

The huge number of Manchester United fans is another reason the team is so popular. Manchester United has fans in at least twenty-four countries.

Many fans around the world join Manchester United Supporters Clubs. These clubs get together to watch games and cheer on their favorite team.

The club is also popular on social media sites. In fact, it has the third-highest following worldwide out of all sports teams. In a fun but not-so-scientific study, its fans have been rated the loudest in the Premier League, according to a smartphone app that rated the volume of cheering in the stadium in 2014.

Manchester United is also known for its rivalries with other English clubs. Some of their biggest rivals are Liverpool, Arsenal, Manchester City, and Leeds United. Rivalries can be good, since they help make the team

Manchester United fans are known for their passion. Some, like those shown here, watch their games in person, but others watch from different countries around the world!

This aerial view shows the size of Old Trafford, the home of Manchester United, in the Greater Manchester area.

want to win games. After all, the goal of the game is to win! And winning is certainly something Manchester United has done a lot and does well.

That hasn't always been the case, though. Like any long-running soccer club, Manchester United has had good times and bad times. They've been at the top of their leagues, but they've also been near the bottom.

Learning the history of the club is a fun roller-coaster ride through English soccer over the past 140 years.

SPORT SHORT

One low point in Manchester United's history occurred in February 1958. Eight players were killed in a plane crash, and several others were hurt. Sir Matt Busby, the team's manager, or coach, at the time was among those hurt in the crash.

Manchester United players (in peach) celebrate winning an important match against French team Paris Saint-Germain (in black) in 2019.

The Manchester United team gathers for a picture during the 1911–1912 season.

Manchester United's history goes back a long time. The team is located in the Old Trafford area of Manchester in England. While London is the city most people think of when thinking about England, Manchester is another large area. It's nowhere near London, though. In fact, it's about 200 miles (322 kilometers) north. Manchester, however, has a large number of people and includes many soccer fans!

THE STORY OF THE RED DEVILS

People often wonder how the team got its nickname of "Red Devils." Way back in 1934, a popular rugby team from Salford in Greater Manchester (the main city plus areas around the city) played in a tour in France. French journalists who watched called the Manchester team *Les Diables Rouges*, which means "the Red Devils."

Meanwhile, the Manchester United soccer team had been nicknamed "the Heathens," because the club started in Newton Heath and was the first team

Fred the Red is the mascot of Manchester United.

to play on Sundays. At that time, many people thought Sunday was for going to church and resting, not for playing sports. Those who did play were jokingly called heathens because they were going against the religious day.

In the 1960s, Sir Matt Busby was the team's manager. He reportedly didn't like the nickname the Heathens, so he said that the team would be called the Red Devils. The term had a similar meaning to the Heathens but sounded more frightening. In 1970, a devil was added to the team's jersey badge, and their official mascot became Fred the Red, a devil.

BEFORE THEY WERE DEVILS

Before the club was the Red Devils, and even before they were the Heathens, they were the Newton Heath LYR Football Club. A department, or section, of the Lancashire and York Railway company started the team in 1878.

For the first couple of years, Newton Heath LYR played matches, or games, against teams from other LYR departments and against other railway companies. In late 1880, though, they competed in their first recorded match, losing to the Bolton Wanderers. Back then, they had a very different look—wearing green and gold uniforms.

In the late 1880s, the club was part of a couple of leagues, neither of which lasted long. By the early 1890s, the club had left LYR and was competing as the Newton Heath Football Club in the First Division

SPORT SHORT

Manchester United's home stadium is called Old Trafford. The team has played home games there since 1910. They only stopped playing during and after World War II, partially because many players fought in the war and partially because the stadium was hit by bombs and needed to be fixed.

and Second Division of the English Football League. The First Division, at that time, was the highest level of soccer, while the Second Division was second.

By the early 1900s, the club wasn't doing well. It was in the Second Division and didn't have enough money to survive. It was ordered to liquidate, or cease being a company. That's when team captain, or lead player, Harry Stafford stepped in and began talking to a rich benefactor named John Henry Davies.

Davies and three other local businessmen agreed to put money into the club, and Davies became club president. In return, Davies changed the team's colors to red and white, and he also changed the team's name from Newton Heath to Manchester United. Stafford also stopped being paid for being captain. This meant the team could save some money.

Team secretary James Ernest Mangnall became manager in 1903. With him, the club finished second among Second Division teams in the 1906 season. This let Manchester United move back into the First Division. In 1908, the club won its first league title as part of the First Division. Things were looking up!

SPORT SHORT

The Manchester United club badge, or crest, is red and yellow. It has a ship from the Manchester City Council coat of arms as well as a devil on it.

YO-YOING IN THE EARLY TWENTIETH CENTURY

After winning the 1908 First Division title and under the management of Mangnall, Manchester United had several more wins, including the first Charity Shield, which is now called the Community Shield, in 1908. This match takes place every year between the previous year's Premier League champions and the winners of the FA Cup. The FA Cup is the oldest national soccer competition. Manchester United won the First Division title again in 1911, not long before Mangnall left to manage rival team Manchester City.

Competitive soccer stopped in England from 1915 to 1919, due to World War I, which had started in 1914. Not every country stopped playing games, but England did. Many cities and stadiums in the country were bombed. Play started again in 1919, with Manchester United playing in the First Division. However, by 1922, Manchester United had slid into the Second Division, where the club stayed for several years.

The club bounced between First Division and Second Division then, with the lowest point being a twentieth-place finish (out of twenty-two) in the Second Division in 1934. This constant switching between First and Second Division made many think of the team as a yo-yo club.

Manchester United fell into financial trouble again in the late 1920s, after club president John Henry Davies died and the Great Depression began. The club struggled for a few years, but in 1931, businessman

James Gibson gave money to the club. He became club chairman and held that role until his death in 1951.

THE LEGENDARY MATT BUSBY

Just as competitive soccer had been on hold during World War I, it was also on hold during World War II. Between the war's start in 1939 and its end in 1945, most soccer games in England were not played. Some leagues tried to continue play, but most realized it was too difficult because so many players were fighting in the war.

When the war ended, Manchester United team chairman James Gibson made Matt Busby the club manager. This led to a few important turning points for the club.

Busby had been involved in soccer since he was a teenager. He started his career playing for Manchester City and Liverpool soccer clubs. After World War II, he turned to coaching but didn't like how little control he had as an assistant coach. He accepted James Gibson's offer to manage Manchester United with the hope of having more control over the team.

Busby wanted to control the team, its players, and its training. His approach, while unusual for the time, had excellent results. Under Busby, the club finished second in the league many times. The team also won several league titles and one FA Cup.

Then, in 1958, one of the worst events in the club's history happened. On February 6, the players were celebrating the match they'd played against Red Star, a team from Belgrade. The tie with them meant Manchester United qualified for the semifinal of the

Sir Matt Busby, former manager of Manchester United, poses for a picture on the Old Trafford pitch in 1979, years after his retirement.

European Cup, a popular international competition. Excited, the team was supposed to fly from Yugoslavia to Manchester but stopped in Munich, Germany, to get more fuel. Wintry conditions in Germany made it tough to fly. Not long after a third takeoff try, the plane crashed. Eight players died and several more people were hurt, including Busby. The loss of many players affected the team and its fans.

In the early 1960s, Busby was able to rebuild the team. It went on to win another FA Cup in 1963, as well as two more league titles and a European Cup.

Matt Busby retired in 1969, having managed Manchester United for more than twenty years.

THE BUSBY BABES

When he became manager of Manchester United, Matt Busby knew he wanted the team to have a lot of fresh, new players—and those players were generally teenagers or young adults. He soon started getting younger players to join.

For many, Manchester United was the only team they'd played on, rather than being bought from other clubs. Many came from a junior athletic club that had been formed at Manchester in the late 1930s. Busby was willing to give these younger players a chance. That made them a bit like Busby's children, or "babes."

Under Busby, the Heathens then became known as the Busby Babes. The average player was twenty-two years old. There were many talented players, and sadly, too many of them were killed in the air disaster of 1958.

The Busby Babes pose in 1957, with Sir Matt Busby at far right. Sadly, six of the players in this photo would lose their lives in the Munich air disaster less than a year after this photo was taken.

He returned in 1970 after his replacement, Wilf McGuinness, was fired. However, he retired from managing completely in 1971. He was the club director and became club president in 1980. He was president until 1993 and passed away in 1994.

YO-YO YEARS AFTER BUSBY

In the years that followed Busby leaving, Manchester United went through several managers. First was Wilf McGuinness, then Busby again, followed by Frank O'Farrell and then Tommy Docherty. McGuinness and O'Farrell lasted a short time, but Docherty was the team's manager for about five years. During Docherty's time, the club continued to yo-yo between First Division and Second Division.

After Docherty, Dave Sexton managed for four years, but the team saw poor season finishes. Under Ron Atkinson, who managed the Red Devils from 1981 to 1986, the team won two FA Cups. During Atkinson's last year, the team was expected to win the league title but finished fourth instead and found itself in danger of slipping once more to the Second Division. Atkinson was then fired.

ALEX FERGUSON STEPS IN

Manchester United finally gained a steady manager again in Sir Alexander Chapman Ferguson. He joined the team in 1986. The team struggled for the first few years under him, but by 1991, the Red Devils were strong once more. In 1993, they won their first league title since the Busby years, and in 1994, they won a

RIVALRIES ON THE PITCH

As much as sports are fun to watch, they are also places where deep rivalries happen. Rivalries can add to the fun, if different sides joke with each other, but they can also lead to violence.

One of Manchester United's biggest and longest-standing rivalries is with Liverpool, a city 45 miles (72 kilometers) away. During the Industrial Revolution, Manchester was known for textiles while Liverpool had many ships docking at their ports. Merchants in Manchester had to pay high fees to import and export their textiles overseas, so they decided to build a large canal, known as the Manchester Ship Canal. The canal would let them reach the open sea without using Liverpool's ports. When it opened in 1894, it was the largest ship canal in the world. It brought attention to the merchants' unhappiness at the high fees. This also caused bad feelings from the citizens of Liverpool, and the rivalry between the two cities has existed ever since.

On the soccer field, though, the two cities happen to have two of English soccer's most successful clubs. Between the two, they have claimed thirty-eight league titles, thirty-six Charity/Community Shields, nineteen FA Cups, one FIFA Club World Cup, and many more awards as of 2019. It's not surprising, then, that these two historic cities would extend their rivalry to the pitch!

With manager Alex Ferguson at center, the Manchester United team celebrates their UEFA Champions League final win in 1999.

second league title and the FA Cup, which is known as winning the double, or doubling, in soccer.

Manchester United doubled again in the 1995–1996 season, under Ferguson's leadership. In the 1998–1999 season, the Red Devils took it a step further by securing a treble—a win of the Premier League title, the FA Cup, and the Union of European Football Associations (UEFA) Champions League final.

Throughout the early 2000s, Manchester United won many league titles, FA Cups, Football League Cups, Community Shields, and the FIFA Club World Cup. In mid-2013, Ferguson retired as the team's manager; however, he stayed on as a director and club ambassador.

MANCHESTER UNITED AFTER FERGUSON

In the years since Ferguson's retirement, the Red Devils have gone through a series of managers. Their performance has been spotty, or good sometimes and bad others. In 2014, they missed out on qualifying for a European competition for the first time in more than two decades and have not won a league title since Ferguson left. However, they have won the FA Cup, an English Football League Cup, and the Community Shield.

If Manchester United has shown the soccer world anything over its history, it's that it's a team of fighters who come out on top. The club may be finding its footing as it searches for another leader, but Manchester United will likely rise to success again.

Manchester United won the Barclays Premier League at Old Trafford in 2013. Here, player Robin van Persie holds up the trophy.

AN OFFERING OF AWARDS AND ACCOLADES

Manchester United has won many trophies and awards. The team usually is the top English club in terms of trophies won. Their biggest rivals, Liverpool, follow closely. In terms of awards in European soccer in general, both teams have been passed—though not by much—by Barcelona and Real Madrid (from Spain) and Bayern Munich (from Germany). Juventus (from Italy) sneaks into the list around the same place as Manchester United and Liverpool—in 2018, they were right between the two English rivals. Earning more trophies and accomplishments helps boost the team's reputation and makes more excitement for fans too.

LEAGUE TITLES

While some soccer fans might not think smaller trophies matter as much as big trophies, a league title win is a big deal. That is particularly true when a team is in the First Division/Premier League, the highest level of play in the English Football League. Manchester United has been considered a yo-yo club, though in recent years, it has spent its time in the Premier League.

It was as a member of the First Division that Manchester United won its first league title in 1908. Since then, the Red Devils have won a record-breaking twenty titles in the First Division and Premier League. Five of those titles were under Matt Busby, and thirteen were under Alex Ferguson. It seems that the Devils play at their best when a strong manager is leading them.

Manchester United players are shown here holding the Premiership trophy the team won in 1997.

Since 2013, the team hasn't had a long-term manager, and while it has won a few cups, it hasn't won a Premier League title. It did, however, win the UEFA Europa League title in 2017. The Europa League was founded in 1971. Teams have to qualify to participate, usually by being a runner-up in their country's top league or by winning the main cup. Manchester United qualified in 2017 by winning the English Football League (EFL) Cup that year.

SPORT SHORT

Manchester United won its first trophy eight years after the team was formed. In 1886, when it was still called Newton Heath LYR, the club won the Manchester Cup.

Not to be confused with the UEFA Europa League title is the UEFA Champions League, previously called the European Cup. This title is one of the most desired in European soccer and worldwide. It is usually played by league champions from each country, though for some countries, the runner-up teams play too. As of summer 2019, Manchester United has won this title three times, most recently in 2008.

The combination of these two titles with the win of one other cup—the European Cup Winners' Cup—makes Manchester United the fifth club in history to win the European treble. Three of the other clubs to earn this distinction are from Italy, Germany, and the Netherlands—Chelsea is the only other English soccer club to earn this honor.

CUP WINS

Only English soccer teams compete for the FA Cup. Manchester United first claimed the FA Cup in 1909, the year after they won their first league title. Since then, they have won twelve FA Cups, most recently in 2016.

Similarly, the Red Devils claimed the League Cup in 2017. This honor is more officially known as the EFL Cup, and it's another famous English soccer competition.

FA COMMUNITY SHIELD

One fun cup is the Football Association Community Shield, previously called the Charity Shield. This competition takes place each year between the team holding the Premier League title for the previous season and the FA Cup winner. If the two competitors happen to be the same team, then the Premier League runner-up plays the Premier League title holder. The Community Shield started in 1908 and is considered a super cup, which means it typically starts a season.

The Football Association organizes the Community Shield each year, and funds from it go to charities around England. Many of the charities are chosen by the clubs that compete in the FA Cup. Past recipients of donations from the Community Shield revenue include cancer research charities, HIV/AIDS charities, mental health awareness projects, eldercare services, and children's charities.

As of 2019, Manchester United has won the Community Shield more times than any other team, with twenty-one individual or shared wins since first winning in 1908.

Manchester United is shown here playing in a Community Shield match against Leicester City in 2016.

Manchester United player Norman Whiteside shows off the FA Cup the team won in 1985 after winning the final against Everton.

It began in 1960, but Manchester United didn't win it until 1992. The team has since won it five times, including its 2017 victory.

Cup competitions don't only exist within a country—there are also international cup competitions. Manchester United won its first international cup in 1999, with a win of the Intercontinental Cup, a competition that ran between 1960 and 2004. The Red Devils played in the Intercontinental Cup only twice and were beaten in their first effort. However, in 1999, they won in a 1–0 match over Brazilian club Palmeiras.

Another international cup is the FIFA Club World Cup. This is not the World Cup that happens once every four years between national teams. It is a lesser event that started in 2000. Winners of a continent's highest competition compete to win the Club World Cup. Only three English soccer clubs have played in it: Manchester United, Liverpool, and Chelsea. Liverpool and Chelsea were both runners-up in their years (2005 and 2012, respectively), but Manchester United claimed the cup in 2008, with a 1–0 win over Ecuadorian club LDU Quito.

DOUBLES AND TREBLES

Doubles and trebles are basically combination wins. A double means a team has won two high-level cups or titles, and a treble means it's won three. Manchester United won the European treble in 2017. The team also won the Continental treble in 1999. That means it won a league title, the FA Cup, and the UEFA Champions League.

The Red Devils have won a number of doubles too. They have won the Premier League and FA Cup double twice, in 1994 and 1996. In 2008, they claimed the European double, which is a win of the Premier League title and the UEFA Champions League. The next year, they claimed a double with the Premier League title and also the EFL League Cup. In 2017, they claimed another double by winning the EFL League Cup and the Europa League title.

Even though there have been changes in management, the club has continued to be a strong team and opponent. It will be fun to see the club continue its monumental success in the future.

WHAT ABOUT THE WOMEN?

While professional men's teams often draw the most lucrative deals with sponsors, a number of sports have successful women's divisions and teams. They may not get the television airtime that the men's teams do, but they are also noteworthy. In 2018, Manchester United started the Manchester United Women Football Club. They practice and play not far from the men's club in Greater Manchester.

This isn't the first time Manchester United has had a women's team, however. A club existed years before, but team owners wanted to focus on youth soccer and so discontinued it. The decision was not liked by many, including the Football Association. It had hoped to expand women's football and was disappointed to see this club go.

As of the 2019 season, the new women's team was in the second level of English women's soccer.

The Manchester United Women team poses for a group picture in 2019. (back row, left to right: Jess Sigsworth, Amy Turner, Ella Toone, Leah Galton, Siobhan Chamberlain, and Alex Greenwood; front row, left to right: Charlie Devlin, Katie Zelem, Mollie Green, Millie Turner, and Kirsty Smith)

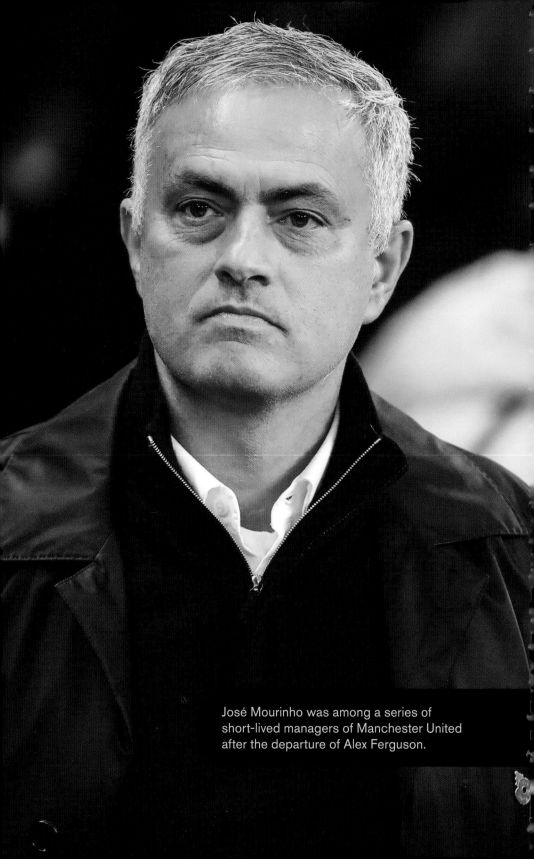

José Mourinho was among a series of short-lived managers of Manchester United after the departure of Alex Ferguson.

CHALLENGES FOR THE CLUB

Although Manchester United has had many wins as a Premier League team, it has also had challenges in its history. Some of the worst include difficulties with money, player deaths, and challenges finding managers.

FINANCIAL CHALLENGES

It's easy to think of soccer as just a sport, but it is also a business. Each team needs businesspeople to run the club, to make financial decisions, and to keep bringing fans and players into stadiums. One person or a group of people can own the team, but it takes many to make sure the team runs well. Many teams go through difficult times, including Manchester United.

Back when the club began as Newton Heath LYR, the money to start the club came from the Lancashire and Yorkshire Railway Company. In 1892, the club began to sell shares, or portions of the ownership in the club bought for a fee, to local fans and supporters. Each share bought was a piece of the team, so a fan who bought one share owned a tiny piece of the team. A fan

Manchester United player Bobby Charlton (*left*) shoots into the goal during a match with Wolverhampton Wanderers.

who bought many shares earned a much bigger piece of the team.

That helped the club a little, but it wasn't enough. In 1902, it was sold to four local businessmen. Each man paid £500 (£59,869 or $78,141 in 2019) for the team. One of these businessmen was John Henry Davies, who was the club president until he died in 1927.

After that, Manchester United struggled again until 1931, when James W. Gibson put £2,000 (£132,722 or $173,228 in 2019) into the club. The Gibson family owned the club for a number of years, even after James Gibson's death. Gibson's shares passed to his wife, Lillian, when he died.

In 1958, the Manchester United plane crash happened, and the club found itself in financial trouble again. At the time, Matt Busby was managing the team. His friend, Louis Edwards, was on the club's board of directors. The board makes a lot of decisions about the team.

Edwards began buying shares of the team. Soon, he owned 54 percent of the club. The people who own the most shares of the club get the biggest say in decisions. Edwards's large number of shares meant he could take control of Manchester United in 1964.

Even though Louis Edwards owned 54 percent of the club's shares, Lillian Gibson still owned a lot too. When she died in 1971, she passed her shares to her son. He sold them to Louis Edwards's son, which meant that the Edwards family then owned even more of the club. A couple of interested people tried to buy out Edwards in the 1980s, but the sales did not happen.

In 1991, Manchester United became traded on the stock exchange. The stock exchange is public, which means that anyone can buy shares of a company on the exchange. When soccer club ownership is set up in this way, it is a publicly traded club. (When a small group of people owns the club, it's called being privately held.)

In 1998, a businessman named Rupert Murdoch tried to take over the club. He bid £623 million (more than £1 billion or almost $1.4 billion in 2019) to own it, but the deal was stopped. Murdoch's attempted takeover, however, did help start what is now known as the Manchester United Supporters' Trust. This is a group that helps fans take control of the club they support by gathering together their shares.

SPORT SHORT

In 1995, Manchester United set the Premier League record for the biggest win when they beat Ipswich Town. The final score was incredible: 9–0. During that same match, Manchester United's Andy Cole made a Premier League record of five goals in one game.

SHIRT SPONSORSHIPS

Soccer clubs bring in money by selling tickets; by offering merchandise like jerseys, hats, or stadium photographs; and through investments. Another

Manchester United's Juan Mata is seen here wearing a jersey with the Chevrolet logo on it. General Motors is a recent shirt sponsor for the team.

way they get money is by having sponsorships. In sponsorships, outside companies make deals with a club in exchange for money. Sponsorship logos can appear on player jerseys, around the stadium, or in TV advertisements.

Manchester United's first shirt sponsor was Sharp Electronics in 1982, and that sponsorship went on for eighteen years. A shirt sponsor is a company that gives a soccer team money in exchange for the team wearing the company's logo on the team shirts. Between 2000 and 2006, the team was sponsored by Vodafone, a British telecommunications company. Starting in late 2006, the team was sponsored by AIG, an American insurance company. The sponsorship was for roughly £56 million (over $103 million). It was the biggest shirt sponsorship deal up to that time. When the AIG sponsorship ended in 2010, Aon, a British company, sponsored Manchester United for an even larger £80 million (more than $130 million).

Up until 2011, Manchester United's shirt sponsorships were all for their home uniforms. However, in 2011, the club accepted a £40 million (almost $62 million) sponsorship for their traveling, or away, uniforms.

If someone were again to try to take over Manchester United, Supporters' Trust members would bring their money together to buy enough shares to stop the takeover. The Manchester United Supporters' Trust is not the only supporters' trust, but it is the largest one in the United Kingdom.

The club's money problems did not end when the Murdoch takeover was blocked, though. When Alex Ferguson was managing the team, two of his business partners, John Magnier and J. P. McManus, bought Manchester United shares. Eventually, they owned enough shares to try to have Ferguson fired. However, the team board stepped in and encouraged investors to buy enough shares that Magnier and McManus would not have the power to fire Ferguson.

That effort stopped things for a while, but in 2005, American businessman Malcolm Glazer bought Magnier's and McManus's shares. This gave Glazer 28.1 percent of the Manchester United shares, which was enough to gain control of the team. In the weeks that followed, Glazer bought more than 75 percent of the club's shares. This was enough to change Manchester United from a publicly traded club back into a privately held one. By the end of the year, Glazer had control over 98 percent of Manchester United's shares.

Not surprisingly, the Manchester United Supporters' Trust was not happy with this takeover. Glazer first tried to buy the club in 2004, but the Supporters' Trust had demonstrated against the purchase. At the time, the Manchester United board refused Glazer's offer. However, Glazer found another way to buy the club—by buying Magnier's and McManus's shares. This was very disappointing to many Red Devil supporters.

Manchester United is now again traded on the stock exchange, but the Glazer family owns 97 percent of the shares. That means they still have control of the club. Malcom Glazer passed away in 2014, but his six children still own the club shares as of 2019.

TRAGEDY

Financial worries aren't the only problems the club has faced. Manchester United has also dealt with tragedy. The most infamous tragedy that the team has faced was the Munich plane crash in February 1958. The team lost eight players and three staff members in the crash. Of the nine other players involved in the crash, two never played soccer for Manchester United again.

Miraculously, twenty-one out of the forty-four passengers and crew on board survived. Unfortunately, Manchester United suffered heavy losses. Players, staff, and journalists died that day. It was a big blow for the team. One of the dead was player Billy Whelan, a nervous passenger who reportedly said before the third takeoff attempt, "This may be death, but I'm ready"—a sad prediction of his future.

Manager Matt Busby survived the crash but was very badly hurt. He was in the hospital for more than two months, and at times doctors didn't know if he would live. Busby's injuries were so bad that he was not told for several weeks that some of his players had died. Doctors worried if they told him he would be very depressed and not get better. When he did learn about

This photo shows the wreckage from the Munich air disaster, which claimed the lives of twenty-three people.

the players' deaths, Busby felt very guilty because he had pushed for the team to be involved in the European Cup that year. If he hadn't, the team would never have been on the plane. He considered quitting as manager, but his wife convinced him to stay. If he was manager, he could remember the players who had died in the crash. While he recovered, his assistant manager

Jimmy Murphy managed the club. Busby came back as manager the following season, and he stayed until 1969.

MANAGER WOES

The club has not always had such steady management. Between Busby leaving and Alex Ferguson taking the job in 1986, Manchester United went through five different managers. None of them lasted more than five years. Lack of a steady manager can be a challenge for a club; like any organization, soccer clubs run well under strong, steady leadership.

Alex Ferguson took over in 1986 and guided the team well, but when he left in 2013, the club faced more managers with even shorter terms. Between Ferguson's retirement in 2013 and early 2019, the team had five different managers. David Moyes took the position after Ferguson left, but he was dismissed after less than a year.

Next up was Ryan Giggs, who had the position for a month. Louis van Gaal took over in July 2014. He signed a three-year contract but didn't last two full years before being fired. Van Gaal had signed several expensive and promising players, but the team didn't perform as well as hoped. This led to him being asked to leave the club.

Former Chelsea manager José Mourinho did slightly better. He arrived in May 2016 and lasted until December 2018. His contract, like van Gaal's, was for three years, and he left before completing it. This was likely due to Manchester United's sixth-place position in the Premier League at the time.

MODERN RIVALRIES

Manchester United and Chelsea have a relatively new rivalry, on display in a 2019 match shown here.

The rivalry between Manchester United and Liverpool continues today, but Manchester United has newer rivalries too. For example, Chelsea has become a tough rival for the Red Devils. When Alex Ferguson still managed Manchester United, José Mourinho was managing Chelsea. The two men were constantly trying to get their clubs in a top position.

Interestingly, Chelsea was not always well liked. This meant that some teams showed their support for Manchester United whenever the two clubs played each other. Even Liverpool supported Manchester United in winning against Chelsea!

Another rivalry is between Manchester United and Arsenal, another Premier League team. The rivalry is rumored to have started in 1990, when players on both teams got into a fight on the field. Manchester United player Denis Irwin was battling Arsenal player Anders Limpar for the ball, and Limpar's teammate tackled Irwin. This caused nearly all the players on both teams to fight each other. The fight was quickly broken up, but the Football Association punished and fined them. The clubs have been rivals ever since.

Manchester United has had many English managers and a few from other countries. However, neither of the club's two longest-running managers are English. Both Matt Busby and Alex Ferguson were from Scotland!

Ole Gunnar Solskjaer was named interim, or in-between, manager at the end of 2018. The choice was interesting because Solskjaer was also the manager of Norwegian club Molde. However, Solskjaer was a former Manchester United striker. He'd played eleven seasons with the club when Alex Ferguson had been the team's manager. He was also popular with Red Devil fans.

Solskjaer was happy to be back with Manchester United. He also wanted Manchester United players to be excited about playing again. His enthusiasm and history with the club lifted team spirits. Under Solskjaer's management, the team performed very well, and in early 2019, he was offered a three-year contract to manage the team.

Manchester United player Chris Smalling (*right*) battles Wolverhampton Wanderer Diogo Jota (*left*) in a 2019 match.

MANCHESTER UNITED'S FUTURE

Manchester United has a long and great history, and the future is wide open for this club. While in recent years a series of managers has joined and quickly left the club, there's hope that a permanent manager will bring more stability to the club.

MANAGEMENT AT MANCHESTER UNITED

When Ole Gunnar Solskjaer became interim manager in 2018 after José Mourinho, some people were very happy to hear the news. Some think Solskjaer is the best striker Manchester United has ever had. He scored 126 goals during his eleven seasons with the club. When Solskjaer was a player, he was often put in an important game to score goals. His late goal at the 1999 UEFA Champions League final meant Manchester United won the treble. It is considered one of the greatest moments in soccer. In other words, Solskjaer had a long history of coming in at the last minute to help out Manchester United.

Ole Gunnar Solskjaer (*right*) played many games for Manchester United during his time with the club.

Solskjaer started out strong in the manager's seat. The club won its first six games under his management. That was the first time such a winning streak had happened since Matt Busby became manager in 1945. Solskjaer was also the first Manchester United manager since Alex Ferguson to win the Premier League Manager of the Month award. In January 2019, Solskjaer told sports journalists that he did not want to leave Manchester United after his interim contract ended in mid-2019. Manchester United clearly felt the same way. In March 2019, Solskjaer was offered a three-year contract to continue managing the team.

PLAYERS TO WATCH WITH MANCHESTER UNITED

Strong team management is a key to soccer success, but the players are important too. Without talent on the field, a team won't do very well. In the twenty-first century, Manchester United has had some major soccer stars on its team, including Wayne Rooney, David Beckham, and Cristiano Ronaldo. Looking to future seasons, Manchester United has several players who are considered ones to watch. Going into the 2019 FA Cup, sports journalists pointed to Paul Pogba, Marcus Rashford, Ander Herrera, David de Gea, and Victor Lindelof as strong players that rival clubs needed to worry about.

One of Manchester United's stars in the 2008–2009 season was Cristiano Ronaldo, shown here in a Premier League match against Arsenal.

Paul Pogba, from France, was a midfielder who played for the Red Devils in the 2011–2012 season. He then spent four years with Juventus before returning to Manchester United in 2016. Pogba showed great talent as a youth player. He later received the Golden Boy Award in 2013 and the Bravo Award in 2014. He helped France win in the 2018 FIFA World Cup after scoring in the finals. In his first twelve games playing under Solskjaer's management, Pogba scored seven goals and assisted on five others.

Marcus Rashford, from England, joined as a forward for Manchester United in 2015. He also played for Manchester United's youth division between 2005 and 2015. He definitely has a long history with the club! Rashford has an impressive scoring history. He scored goals in his first League Cup match, his first UEFA

Paul Pogba settles the ball on the pitch during a Premier League match against the Wolverhampton Wanderers in 2019.

Champions League match, and his first Manchester derby (competition between Manchester United and Manchester City). Rashford was also the youngest English player to score in his first senior international match. As of early 2019, Rashford had scored forty-three goals in his first four seasons for the Premier League—an impressive debut! He has continued that trend under Solskjaer's management.

Ander Herrera Agüera, from Spain, came to Manchester United in 2014. He played as a midfielder for the club. Before his arrival, he played six seasons for different Spanish clubs. He also played for the Spanish national team. Herrera was an intense player whose style of play was comparable to Manchester United legendary midfielder Paul Scholes. (Scholes played for nearly twenty years under manager Alex Ferguson.)

A team is nothing without a strong defense. Many think Manchester United's strongest defender is Victor Lindelof from Sweden. He came to Manchester United in 2017 on a four-year contract after playing for several Swedish clubs. Lindelof is a strong defender who usually played center-back or right-back. However, under Solskjaer's management, Lindelof has moved

Manchester United goalie David de Gea is shown here. He is wearing a green jersey to be easily identifiable as the goalie.

into the midfield when needed. This has made him a double threat!

Then there is David de Gea, who is originally from Spain. De Gea became Manchester United's goalkeeper in 2011. He is thought to be one of the world's best goalkeepers. He is known for fast reflexes, impressive agility, and the ability to make saves not only with his hands and body, but also with his feet. When needed, de Gea also acted as a sweeper-keeper, rushing off the goal line for one-on-one defense. If opposing teams made it past defenders like Victor Lindelof, they would still have to face down de Gea.

With all this talent and a strong manager on board, Manchester United seems to be in the running for the top club in English soccer for quite some time. It will be interesting to follow the team into the future.

CHRONOLOGY

1878 Manchester United is founded as Newton Heath LYR Football Club.

1886 Newton Heath wins its first trophy, the Manchester Cup.

1902 Newton Heath changes its name to Manchester United and adopts red, white, and black colors for uniforms after being purchased by four businessmen.

1908 Manchester United wins its first league title.

1909 Manchester United wins its first FA Cup.

1910 Manchester United moves into Old Trafford stadium, the team's current home.

1945 Matt Busby is appointed club manager.

1958 The Munich air disaster takes the lives of eight Manchester United players and injures more players and coaches, including manager Matt Busby.

1969 Matt Busby resigns as club manager.

1986 Alex Ferguson is appointed club manager.

1991 Manchester United's stock is offered on the London Stock Exchange.

1999 Manchester United wins the Continental treble.

2005 Malcolm Glazer purchases the club, making it once again privately held.

2008   Manchester United wins the FIFA Club
        World Cup.

2012   Manchester United's stock is offered on
        the New York Stock Exchange.

2013   Alex Ferguson retires as club manager.

2017   Manchester United wins the
        European treble.

2018   Ole Gunnar Solskjaer is named
        interim manager.

2019   Ole Gunnar Solskjaer is offered
        a three-year contract to manage
        Manchester United.

GLOSSARY

benefactor A person who gives money to a cause.

brand The identity of a team or a group that helps set it apart from other teams or groups in terms of marketing.

crest A design that stands for a group or team and is used on a team's uniforms or in the stadium.

derby Games between two local rival teams, such as Manchester United vs. Manchester City.

double The achievement of winning a country's primary cup and also its top-level division in the same season.

earnings Money that is given in exchange for work or services.

final The last game in a competition.

Great Depression The long economic downturn that came about after the stock market crashed in 1929.

heathen A person who does not follow a religion.

liquidate To end a business and convert its assets into cash by selling them.

manager The person in charge of the play and training of a sports team.

pitch In British English, a playing field.

privately held Owned by a small number of shareholders and not offering stock on the stock exchanges.

publicly held Relating to a business with ownership split among the general public through shares traded on the stock exchange.

rivalry A competition between two groups, people, or teams.

rugby A sport popular in England that is similar to football and soccer.

semifinal The second-to-last game in a competition.

shares Equal parts into which a company's value is divided.

sponsorship A deal in which an entity gives financial support to a team or athlete in exchange for the team or athlete's promotion of their brand.

takeover The act of one entity taking over another by buying up shares of the company.

treble The achievement of winning three particular competitions in soccer.

yo-yo club A club that swings between multiple leagues of play, such as Premier League vs. Second Division.

FURTHER INFORMATION

BOOKS

French, Paul. *A Brief History of Soccer: From Victorian Britain to a Global Phenomenon*. Surrey, UK: Digiteller Publishing, 2018.

Ignotofsky, Rachel. *Women in Sports: 50 Fearless Athletes Who Played to Win*. San Francisco, CA: Ten Speed Press, 2017.

Luke, Andrew. *History of the Cup*. Broomall, PA: Mason Crest, 2018.

Oldfield, Matt, and Tom Oldfield. *De Gea: Ultimate Football Heroes*. London, UK: Dino Books, 2019.

WEBSITES

English Football League

https://www.efl.com

The EFL website has a vast amount of information about the clubs that make up the league.

FIFA Club World Cup

https://www.fifa.com/clubworldcup

The official Club World Cup website has anything and everything you want to know about the Club World Cup and the teams playing in it.

Manchester United

https://www.manutd.com

The official website of Manchester United is a one-stop shop for facts about all things related to the Red Devils.

Sky Sports

https://www.skysports.com/football

Sky Sports is a great website for many sports, but their soccer/football page will keep readers up to date about the latest and greatest soccer news.

VIDEOS

England

https://www.youtube.com/channel/UCNT2e7Og56vm5_V-yJWvglA

The English national soccer team has a YouTube channel with videos of some of the most exciting matches.

Manchester United YouTube Page

https://www.youtube.com/channel/UC6yW44UGJJBvYTlfC7CRg2Q

Manchester United has a YouTube page with numerous interviews and videos.

2018 Club World Cup Final

https://www.youtube.com/watch?v=wm-bYT6fC7Y

Watch clips from Manchester United's exciting 2008 Club World Cup victory.

SELECTED BIBLIOGRAPHY

Bloomfield, Craig. "Which Club Has Won the Most Trophies in Europe? The Most Successful Clubs from the Best Leagues Revealed." TalkSport. August 13, 2015. https://talksport.com/football/fa-cup/312381/which-club-has-won-most-trophies-europe-most-successful-clubs-best-leagues-revealed/.

Cunningham, John M. "Why Do Some People Call Football 'Soccer'?" Encyclopedia Britannica. Accessed March 26, 2019. https://www.britannica.com/story/why-do-some-people-call-football-soccer.

Farrell, Dom. "Solskjaer on His Man United Future: I Don't Want to Leave!" Goal.com. January 2, 2019. https://www.goal.com/en/news/solskjaer-on-his-man-united-future-i-dont-want-to-leave/1ikk5dr4c5zgn1tqsbntmsj8q2.

"From Matt Busby to Jose Mourinho – Manchester United Managers in Pictures." National. December 19, 2018. https://www.thenational.ae/sport/football/from-matt-busby-to-jose-mourinho-manchester-united-managers-in-pictures-1.804299#12.

"Glazer Gets 98% of Man Utd Shares." BBC News. June 28, 2005. http://news.bbc.co.uk/2/hi/business/4629401.stm.

"History of Football – The Origins." FIFA.com. Accessed March 26, 2019. https://www.fifa.com/about-fifa/who-we-are/the-game.

Jackman, Spencer. "World Cup vs. Super Bowl By the Numbers: Viewers, Revenue, Ratings." The 18. May 5, 2018. https://the18.com/soccer-news/world-cup-vs-super-bowl-by-numbers-viewers-revenue-tv-ratings.

Leighton, Tony. "United Abandon Women's Game to Focus on Youth." Guardian. February 20, 2005. https://www.theguardian.com/football/2005/feb/21/newsstory.sport2.

"Manchester United Fans the Premier League's Loudest, Says Study." ESPN.com. November 24, 2014. http://www.espn.com/soccer/league-name/story/2162036/headline.

"Manchester United vs Chelsea: A Rivalry That Will Not Die." April 3, 2010. *Independent*. https://www.independent.co.uk/sport/football/premier-league/manchester-united-vs-chelsea-a-rivalry-that-will-not-die-1934609.html.

Nakrani, Sachin, and Jamie Jackson. "Glazers Do Not Intend to Sell Manchester United Amid Reports of Saudi Interest." *Guardian*. October 21, 2018. https://www.theguardian.com/football/2018/oct/21/glazer-family-have-no-immediate-intention-to-sell-manchester-united.

Odhiambo, Cyril. "FA Cup 2018-19: 4 Manchester United Players to Watch Out for Against Chelsea." Sportskeeda. February 15, 2019. https://www.sportskeeda.com/football/fa-cup-4-manchester-united-players-to-watch-out-for-vs-chelsea.

"Ole Gunnar Solskjaer: Man Utd Caretaker Boss Will 'Get Players Enjoying Football' Again." BBC Sport. December 20, 2018. https://www.bbc.com/sport/football/46640577.

Shah, Rushabh. "5 Amazing Facts You Probably Wouldn't Know About Manchester United." Sportskeeda. Accessed March 26, 2019. https://www.sportskeeda.com/football/five-amazing-facts-probably-wouldn-t-know-manchester-united/4.

Street, Sam. "Deal with the Devil: Why Are Manchester United Called the Red Devils, When Did the Nickname Start and Is It Used Officially?" *Sun*. November 21, 2016. https://www.thesun.co.uk/sport/2230315/why-are-manchester-united-called-the-red-devils-when-did-the-nickname-start-and-is-it-used-officially.

"30 Most Successful Football Clubs Worldwide." Footy Headlines. May 15, 2018. https://www.footyheadlines.com/2018/05/here-are-clubs-with-most-trophies-in-the-world.html.

INDEX

Page numbers in **boldface** are images.

Arsenal, 9, 46, **51**

benefactor, 16
brand, 8
Busby, Sir Matt, 10, 14, 18–20, **19**, **21**, 22, 28, 38, 43–45, 47, 50

crest, 16

Davies, John Henry, 16–17, 38
de Gea, David, 51, 54, **54**
derby, 53
double, 22, 24, 33

earnings, 8
Europa League, 28–29, 33
European Cup, 18–19, 29, 44

FA Cup, 7, 17–19, 22–25, 29–30, **32**, 33, 51
Fédération Internationale de Football Association (FIFA), 7
Ferguson, Sir Alexander, 22–25, **24**, 28, 42, 45–47, 50, 53
FIFA Club World Cup, 23–24, 33
final, 24, 39, 49, 52
First Division, 15–17, 22, 27–28
Football Association (FA), 6–7, 30, 34, 46
football vs. soccer, 5–6
Fred the Red, **14**, 15

Great Depression, 17

heathen, 13–15, 20

International Football Association Board (IFAB), 7

Leeds United, 9
Lindelof, Victor, 51, 53–54
liquidate, 16

Liverpool, 9, 18, 23, 27, 33, 46

manager, 10, 14, 16, 18, 20, 22, 24–25, 28, 37, 44–45, 47, 49–50, 53–54
Manchester City, 9, 16–18, 53
Mourinho, José, **36**, 45–46, 49

Newton Heath LYR, 8, 14–16, 28, 37

Old Trafford stadium, **10**, 15, **19**

pitch, **19**, 23, **52**
Pogba, Paul, 51–52, **52**
Premier League, 7, 9, 17, 24, 27–30, 33, 37, 39, 46–47, 50, 53
privately held, 39, 42
publicly held, 39, 42

Red Devils, 8, 13–15, 22, 24–25, 28–29, 32–33, 46, 52
rivalry, 23, 46, 53
Ronaldo, Cristiano, 51, **51**
rugby, 6, 13
Rugby Football Union, 6

semifinal, 18, 43
shares, 37–39, 42–43
Solskjaer, Ole Gunnar, 47, 49–50, **50**, 52–53
sponsorship, 40–41

takeover, 39, 42
treble, 24, 29, 33, 49

UEFA Champions League, 24, 29, 33, 49
Union of European Football Associations (UEFA), 24, 29

World Cup, 5, 33
World War I, 17–18
World War II, 15, 18

yo-yo club, 17, 27

ABOUT THE AUTHOR

Cathleen Small is the author of more than sixty books for children and teens, on topics ranging from sports to politics to technology. Her interest in soccer comes from her nine years spent playing defense in youth soccer. When she's not writing, Small enjoys traveling and hanging out with her two sons. She and her family reside in the San Francisco Bay Area.